DINOSAURS AND THEIR DISCOVERERS™

The First Dinosaur Eggs and Roy Chapman Andrews

Brooke Hartzog

The Rosen Publishing Group's
PowerKids Press™
New York

Published in 1999 by The Rosen Publishing Group, Inc.
29 East 21st Street, New York, NY 10010

First Edition

Book Design: Danielle Primiceri

Photo Credits: pp. 4, 14 © Hulton-Deutsch Collection/Corbis; p. 5 © 1997 Digital Vision ltd.; p. 6 © Telegraph Colour Library/FPG International; pp. 9, 17 © Barry Rosenthal/FPG International; p. 10 © Hulton Getty/Tony Stone Images; p. 13 © UPI/Corbis-Bettmann; p. 18 © Kevin Schafer/Corbis; pp. 21, 22 © American Museum of Natural History.

Hartzog, Brooke.
    The first dinosaur eggs and Roy Chapman Andrews / by Brooke Hartzog.
       p.   cm.—(Dinosaurs and their discoverers)
    Includes index.
    Summary: Describes the expeditions led by Roy Andrews for New York's American Museum of Natural History to the Gobi Desert in Mongolia in an effort to uncover dinosaur fossils.
    ISBN 0-8239-5329-7
    1. Andrews, Roy Chapman, 1884–1960—Juvenile literature. [1. Andrews, Roy Chapman, 1884–1960. 2. Naturalists. 3. Paleontology.] I. Title. II. Series: Hartzog, Brooke. Dinosaurs and their discoverers.

QH31.A55H37 1998
567.9'092—dc21
                                              98-10338
                                                CIP
                                                    AC

Contents

A Boy's Dream

When Roy Chapman Andrews was a young boy growing up in Wisconsin, he had a dream. He wanted to work in a natural history **museum** (myoo-ZEE-um).

Roy worked hard to make his dream come true.

4

When Roy wasn't at school, he was **exploring** (ek-SPLOR-ing) the woods near his home. Roy collected rocks and studied them. He also studied animals and plants. When he finished college, Roy took a job scrubbing floors at the American Museum of Natural History in New York City. Of course, he wanted to do more than that. But this was the only job he could get. And Roy loved being around the huge dinosaur **skeletons** (SKEL-ih-tunz).

Becoming an Explorer

Roy didn't have to scrub floors for very long. Soon he was going on **expeditions** (EK-spuh-DIH-shunz) with the museum's **cetologists** (see-TAH-loh-jists), or scientists that study whales. Roy and the other scientists often returned to the museum with whale bones. He was very excited about this work. Sometimes Roy even crawled into the bellies of these whale skeletons to see what it was really like inside a whale! He spoke about his adventures to anyone who would listen. Many people gave money to the museum. This helped Roy go on more expeditions.

◄ *While working at the museum, Roy became interested in lots of new things, such as whales.*

Fossils in the Desert?

Some of the scientists at the Museum of Natural History had a new idea. Roy and these scientists believed that all the animals in the world came from animals that had lived in Asia millions of years ago. When these ancient animals died, their bodies were covered with layers of **sediment** (SEH-dih-mint). Over the years, the sediment became rock and the remains of these creatures turned into **fossils** (FAH-sulz). The scientists thought that they might find these fossils in the Gobi Desert in Mongolia. Most people thought there were only rocks in the Gobi Desert. But Roy wanted to lead an expedition there to try to find the fossils.

Roy was excited to visit the desert to see if he and the other scientists were right about finding fossils there. ▶

The Journey Begins

In the spring of 1922, Roy started on his journey to the Gobi Desert. Looking for fossils in the Gobi wasn't easy. Five weeks earlier, Roy had sent in a team with 75 camels carrying food, clothing, gasoline, and tents for the team to sleep in at night. More scientists and workers followed the supplies in three cars and two trucks. There weren't any roads going through the desert. Instead, Roy and his team had to use the stars in the night sky to find their way.

Roy and his team brought many supplies because there weren't any stores or hotels in the desert.

Fossils Discovered!

Most deserts are sandy. But the Gobi Desert is rocky. The cars and trucks that followed the camels had to move slowly over the rough ground. It took four days to drive less than 200 miles. On the fourth day, Roy and his team picked a **site** (SYT) to set up camp. There were few plants and no other people around Roy's group. But Roy still thought there might be fossils there. Two of the scientists explored the area near the camp. The scientists came back to the campsite with their pockets full of fossils! Roy Chapman Andrews had been right!

After traveling so far, Roy was glad that he found fossils. ▶

MONGOLIA

The Nomads Wonder

Nomads (NOH-madz) who lived in the Gobi Desert had probably always known fossils were there. But these native people of Mongolia didn't know exactly what the strangely shaped rocks were. And the nomads didn't believe that fossils were the only things that Andrews and his people wanted. The nomads thought the visiting Americans were really looking for gold or oil. Some nomads even thought Roy and his team were **possessed** (puh-ZEST) by evil spirits. The nomads had never seen cars or trucks. Many of the nomads thought the Devil had brought these machines to their desert.

The nomads found it hard to believe that Roy and his team were only looking for old bones and rocks.

Dangers of the Desert

Finding fossils was the easiest part of Roy's expedition. There were many dangers in the Gobi. Roy and his team had to carry guns and knives to protect themselves against wild dogs that lived in the desert. One night, a pack of fourteen dogs was circling Roy's tent. He shot the leader of the pack and killed it. The other dogs ran away. Roy's team also had to watch out for **bandits** (BAN-ditz) who might steal the cars and supplies. And the weather was dangerous too. At night, the **temperature** (TEMP-ruh-chur) could drop far below freezing.

Even when things looked peaceful on an expedition, Roy and his team knew to be on the alert ▶ for hidden dangers.

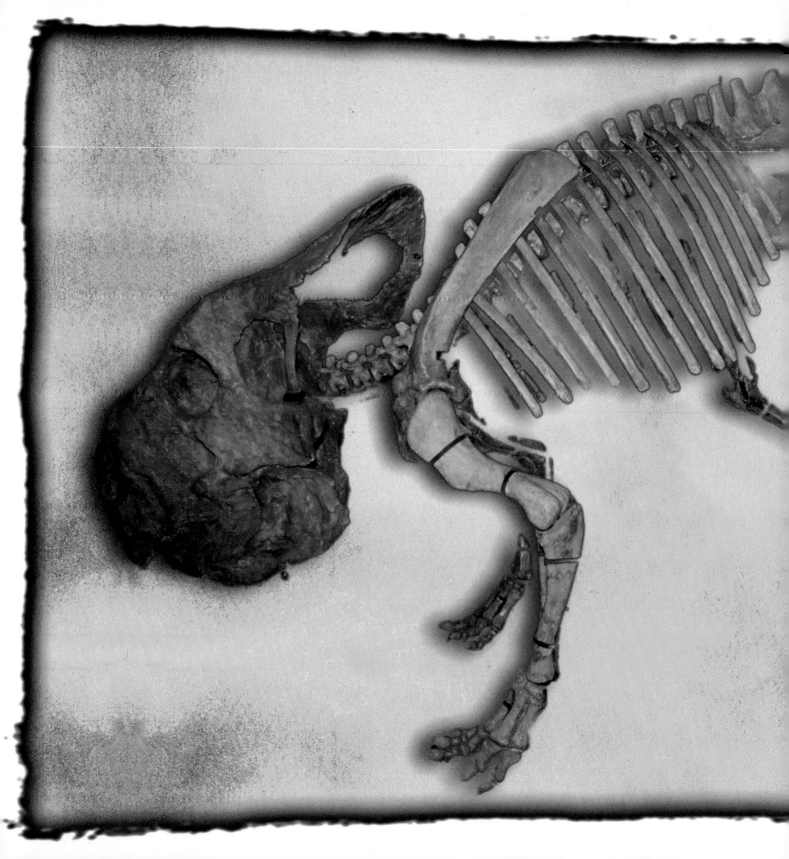

Important Finds

Roy found many important fossils. He found a skull belonging to the largest **mammal** (MA-mul) that ever lived on land. The **indricotherium** (in-DREE-koh-THEER-ee-um) was related to the modern-day rhinoceros. Another discovery was the **ancestor** (AN-ses-ter) of the **triceratops** (try-SEH-ruh-tops). It was named *Protoceratops andrewsi* (proh-toh-SEH-ruh-tops an-DROO-see) in honor of Roy Chapman Andrews. Roy and his team uncovered so many fossils that they had to wrap some of them in clothes or rags when they ran out of packing **material** (muh-TEER-ee-ul)!

◀ *Roy planned to return to the Gobi Desert the next summer to look for more fossils and skeletons.*

Did Dinosaurs Lay Eggs?

Roy returned to the Gobi Desert the following summer. On this second trip, he made his most famous discovery. Roy's favorite place to hunt fossils in the Gobi was called the Flaming Cliffs. It was called Flaming Cliffs because of the beautiful rock shapes there. At Flaming Cliffs, the scientists found several groups of fossils that were shaped like eggs. The fossils looked like they hadn't been touched since they were left in their nest. Roy and his team had discovered the first dinosaur eggs! Some of the eggs were cracked. The scientists were able to see fossilized dinosaur **embryos** (EM-bree-ohz) inside the cracked shells.

The discovery of dinosaur eggs was a big step in dinosaur exploration. Now scientists could learn about dinosaur babies. ▶

Egg-Eating Dinosaurs

Millions of years ago, the Gobi Desert was a swamp. The protoceratops dug nests in the ground and laid eggs there. These were the eggs and nests Roy and his team found. One nest had the skeleton of another kind of dinosaur lying on top of it. The dinosaur's head was crushed. That dinosaur had probably been killed when a protoceratops found the dinosaur eating her eggs. The scientists named this dinosaur **oviraptor** (OH-vih-RAP-ter), which means egg stealer. The discovery of the dinosaur eggs made headlines in newspapers around the world. It also made Roy Chapman Andrews a very famous dinosaur discoverer.

Glossary

ancestor (AN-ses-ter) A relative that lived long ago.

bandit (BAN-dit) A person who steals from travelers.

cetologist (see-TAH-loh-jist) A person who studies whales.

embryo (EM-bree-oh) The form of a baby animal as it grows before birth.

expedition (EK-spuh-DIH-shun) A trip a group takes to find out more about something.

explore (ek-SPLOR) To search for something.

fossil (FAH-sul) The remains of an animal or plant from the past found in Earth's crust.

indricotherium (in-DREE-koh-THEER-ee-um) A huge, four-footed, plant-eating dinosaur that lived millions of years ago.

mammal (MA-mul) An animal that is warm-blooded, breathes oxygen, and gives birth to live young.

material (muh-TEER-ee-ul) A fabric or cloth.

museum (myoo-ZEE-um) A building where historical items are displayed.

nomad (NOH-mad) A person who moves from place to place with no single home.

oviraptor (OH-vih-RAP-ter) A small two-footed dinosaur that lived millions of years ago and ate the eggs of other dinosaurs.

possessed (puh-ZEST) Taken over or ruled by.

Protoceratops andrewsi (proh-toh-SEH-ruh-tops an-DROO-see) A four-footed plant-eating dinosaur that lived millions of years ago. It was one of the last dinosaurs to die out.

sediment (SEH-dih-mint) Gravel or earth carried by wind or water.

site (SYT) The scene of a certain event.

skeleton (SKEL-ih-tun) The set of all the bones in an animal's body.

temperature (TEMP-ruh-chur) How hot or cold something is.

triceratops (try-SEH-ruh-tops) A large plant-eating dinosaur that lived in forests.

Index